P.rn in Kent in 1929, U. A. FANTHORF ...
...enham Ladies' College, and then 'be...
...n order to write', publishing her first collection, *Side Effects*, in
... After working as a hospital clerk in Bristol, she was the Arts
...cil Literary Fellow at Lancaster, and in 1994 she was the first
...n to be nominated for the post of Professor of Poetry at
...l. Her nine volumes of poetry are all published by Peterloo
...her *Selected Poems* was published by Penguin in 1986 and her
...as Poems* were jointly published by Enitharmon Press and
...o Poets in 2002. She has also written children's poetry for
...stal Zoo. U. A. Fanthorpe was awarded the CBE in 2001 and
...ieen's Gold Medal for Poetry in 2003, the same year in which
...llected Poems* (Peterloo) appeared.

...BAILEY was born in Northumberland and has worked as
...eria assistant, librarian, information officer, teacher, counsel-
...nd latterly as director of undergraduate courses in Humanities
...e University of the West of England, Bristol. She is the other
...e in poetry recordings by U. A. Fanthorpe (*Awkward Subject,
Double Act, Poetry Quartets 5*), and has published a pamphlet, *Course
Work* (Culverhay Press, 1997) and a full collection with Peterloo,
Marking Time (2004).

As well as his drawings for U. A. Fanthorpe's *Christmas Poems*,
NICK WADLEY's illustrations include those to accompany prose
...n. poems by Robert Walser, Tom Whalen, John Ashbery, Simon
...chik (2002–7), and for Michael Aalders' *Out to Lunch in Provence
...07). He has exhibited in London, Buenos Aires and Warsaw.

+

U. A. Fanthorpe & R. V. Bailey

From Me to You

Love Poems

Drawings by Nick Wadley

ENITHARMON PRESS

PETERLOO POETS

First published in 2007
by Enitharmon Press
26B Caversham Road
London NW5 2DU

www.enitharmon.co.uk

&
Peterloo Poets
The Old Chapel
Sand Lane
Calstock
Cornwall PL18 9QX

Distributed in the UK by
Central Books
99 Wallis Road
London E9 5LN

Distributed in the USA and Canada
by Dufour Editions Inc.
PO Box 7, Chester Springs
PA 19425, USA

Drawings © Nick Wadley 2007
Text © U.A. Fanthorpe & R.V. Bailey 2007

ISBN: 978-1-904634-55-3 (Enitharmon)
ISBN: 978-1-904324-47-8 (Peterloo)

Enitharmon Press gratefully acknowledges the financial support of
Arts Council England, London.

British Library Cataloguing-in-Publication Data.
A catalogue record for this book is available
from the British Library.

CONTENTS

PREFACE

Our fathers – who never met – grew up in Nottinghamshire, but we were born three hundred miles apart, one in Kent, the other in Northumberland.

We grew up during the Second World War, accustomed to air-raids and bombing, as well the minor dramas of rationing and clothing coupons. One went to Oxford, the other to Cambridge, at a time when there was a very limited intake (the quota) of women students. M. C. Bradbrook, E. M. W. Tillyard, F. R. (and indeed, Queenie) Leavis were among the Cambridge luminaries of those days, while Tolkien, C. S. Lewis and Lord David Cecil were famous at Oxford.

After university we were both in London, where we never came across one another (though we might have done, since one of us lived in the Temple and the other worked just off Fleet Street). We met, at last, in Cheltenham, teaching English in the same school. After seven years it occurred to us that we liked each other, so when we left (one in 1970, the other a year later) we bought our first house together, in Merthyr Tydfil. Eventually, we returned to Gloucestershire, to settle in Wotton-under-Edge, where we have lived since 1975. After a variety of jobs, one became a clerk-receptionist at a Bristol hospital, and the other began work as a university lecturer. It was at that time that the Muse moved in with us; she has been the third member of the household ever since.

FROM ME TO YOU

Wordsworth speaks of the spontaneous overflow of powerful feelings. This seems an apt description of these love poems. They are not important resonant pieces of writing: they simply happened when one of us felt like writing to the other, quite often when one of us was away from home. Some of them coincided with

Valentine's Days or birthdays, but that was more a matter of good luck than foresight.

Quakers, rightly, maintain that Christmas Day is only one important day of all the three hundred and sixty-five important days in the year. It's the same with love poems: they are appropriate at any time, and can be written, incidentally, to dogs, cats, etc., as well as humans.

We haven't indicated which of us wrote which of these poems. In 1934, Sylvia Townsend Warner and Valentine Ackland published their own collection of love poems, *Whether a Dove or a Seagull*, without attributions. This kind of comic modesty seems appropriate.

The pleasant thing about writing such poems, apart from having someone to write them for, is that there is no particular restriction as to the subject matter. In *Christmas Poems*, U. A. felt the draughty awareness of the diminishing cast of subjects, from donkey to Christmas tree. With love, on the other hand, the sky's the limit.

One person whose name must be celebrated is Nick Wadley, most perceptive and witty of illustrators. He has taken our ideas, shaken them out, folded them, and made them fit for society. Another is of course Stephen Stuart-Smith, most generous of publishers, who had the idea in the first place.

UAF & RVB

20.VIII.2003

Today's your birthday. I haven't yet traced
That brilliant solution I've searched for since this time last year.

Ideally I'd give you:

> the county of Devon, sea, valley, hill and moorland;
> all the sheep and cattle of England to rescue from abattoirs;
> true-love collie-cross Polly, miraculously charged with long life;
> half-a-century's supply of Teacher's;
> that rosy-cheeked old housekeeper we used to imagine, ready with
>   meals and understanding (otherwise invisible);
> plenty of room in your sheds;
> a magical librarian, to put the books in order and make them
>   stay put;
> our gardener to come more often, and work for love;
> something to comfort that inner sadness you won't let me
>   tamper with;
> time: to walk, write, paint, be on you own or with friends (this
>   most of all, not wasting it on a Johnnie-head-in-air like me)

However, this is the real world. In it you'll find a bird-feeder,
And have no time to watch birds feeding. In fact,
Like all your other presents, this one seems meant for me.

con amore, et cetera –

9

THE ABSENT-MINDED LOVER'S APOLOGY

I would like you to think I love you *warmly*
Like brown cat yawning among sheets in the linen-cupboard.

I would like you to think I love you *resourcefully*
Like rooftop starlings posting chuckles down the flue.

I would like you to think I love you *extravagantly*
Like black cat embracing the floor when you pick up the
tin opener.

I would like you to think I love you *accurately*
Like Baskerville kern that fits its place to a T.

I would like you to think I love you *with hurrahs and hallelujahs*
Like dog whippetting at you down the intricate hillside.

I would like you to think I love you *wittily*
Like pottery Cox that lurks in the fruitbowl under the Granny
Smiths.

I would like you to think I love you *pacifically and for ever*
Like collared doves on the whitebeam's domestic branch.

I would like you to think I love you *chronically*
Like second hand solemnly circumnavigating the clock.

And O I want to love you, not in the absent tense, *but in the here
and the now*
Like a present-minded lover.

ADJECTIVES FOR U.A.

Brave, excitable, loving, untrustworthy,
Ready to laugh/weep (but readier to laugh);
Ready to sleep, to say Yes thanks;
Readily seduced by the by-ways of coffee, drink, chat;
A straight bat, a dodgy dossier;
Cat-person, crab-person, nipper, water-lover;
Well-meaning, tactless, generous;
Precise, exact, sloppy, idle;
Passionate, absorbed, preoccupied;
Abstracted, scornful, shy,
Cowardly about tricky telephone calls,
Courageous in the ambulance,
The ward, the clinic; tender with frail,
Child, animal, all the lost. And happily

In love with the long-ago lovely English past;
With words, like all of these, and all the others
That one day I will tame to say
How dear you are to me.

ALL I CAN SAY
(14.II.2004)

The tenderness with which you probe
The doubtful places in the skirting board

Scrupulousness with which you scour
The nastier regions of the sink

The way you make a bed, exact,
Elaborate, right as mathematics

The way you prune a bush or mow the lawn
Fastidious and gentle as a surgeon –

I can't keep up with you. My way of doing
Is fumbling, hasty, inexact and wrong.

Can't even love you in the way you do it,
Tender, fastidious, scrupulous, exact.

All I can say is, give me time to learn.
I want to get it right, to echo you.

But I can't even get this simple humble obvious thing to rhyme.

You are   what I would choose

for companion in the desert.
You would know the way out,
think providently about water.

in the solicitor's office.
You would have generous answers
for disagreeable contingencies.

on the motorway.
In your presence
I shouldn't notice tailbacks.

at the picnic.
You would have remembered matches,
have brought a surprise for the greedy.

at the funeral.
You would speak gently with mourners,
but your hands would be warm with life.

Here my four-year-old father opened a gate,
And cows meandered through into the wrong field.

I forgot who told me this. Not, I think,
My sometimes reticent father. Not much I know

About the childhood of that only child. Just
How to pronounce the name, sweetly deceitful

In its blunt spelling, and how Trent
Was his first river. Still here, but the church

Closed now, graveyard long-grassed,
No one to ask in the village. Somewhere here,

I suppose, I have a great-grandfather buried,
Of whom nothing is known but that, dying, he called

My father's mother from Kent to be forgiven.
She came, and was. And came again

To her sister, my great-aunt, for
Her dying pardon too. So my chatty mother,

But couldn't tell what needed so much forgiving,
Or such conclusive journeys to this place.

Your father, pampered only brother
Of many elder sisters, four miles away,

Grew up to scull on this river. My father,
Transplanted, grew up near poets and palaces,

Changed Trent for Thames. Water was in his blood;
In a dry part of Kent his telephone exchange

Was a river's name; he went down to die
Where Arun and Adur run out to the sea.

Your father, going north, abandoned skiffs for cars,
And lived and died on the wind-blasted North Sea shore.
They might have met, two cherished children,
Among nurses and buttercups, by the still silver Trent,

But didn't. That other implacable river, war,
Trawled them both in its heady race

Into quick-march regiments. I don't suppose they met
On any front. They found our mothers instead.

So here I stand, where ignorance begins,
In the abandoned churchyard by the river,

And think of my father, his mother, her father,
Your father, and you. Two fathers who never met,

Two daughters who did. One boy went north, one south,
Like the start of an old tale. Confusions

Of memory rise: rowing, and rumours of war;
And war, and peace; the secret in-fighting

That is called marriage. And children, children,
Born by other rivers, streaming in other directions.

You like the sound of my father. He would
Have loved you plainly, for loving me.

Reconciliation is for the quick, quickly. There isn't enough
Love yet in the world for any to run to waste.

AT THE FERRY

Laconic as anglers, and, like them, submissive,
The grey-faced loiterers on the bank,
Charon, of your river.

They are waiting their turn. Nothing we do
Distracts them much. It was you, Charon, I saw,
Refracted in a woman's eyes.

Patient, she sat in a wheel-chair,
In an X-ray department, waiting for someone
To do something to her,

Given a magazine, folded back
At the problem page: *What should I do*
About my husband's impotence?

Is a registry office marriage
Second-best? I suffer from a worrying
Discharge from my vagina.

In her hands she held the thing obediently;
Obediently moved her eyes in the direction
Of the problems of the restless living,

But her mind deferred to another dimension.
Outward bound, tenderly inattentive, she was waiting,
Charon, for you.

And the nineteen-stone strong man, felled
By his spawning brain, lying still to the sound
Of the DJ's brisk chirrup;

He wasn't listening, either. He was on the lookout
For the flurry of the water as your craft
Comes about in the current.

I saw you once, boatman, lean by your punt-pole
On an Oxford river, in the dubious light
Between willow and water,

Where I had been young and lonely, being
Now loved, and older; saw you in the tender, reflective
Gaze of the living

Looking down at me, deliberate,
And strange in the half-light, saying nothing,
Claiming me, Charon, for life.

ATLAS

There is a kind of love called maintenance,
Which stores the WD40 and knows when to use it;

Which checks the insurance, and doesn't forget
The milkman; which remembers to plant bulbs;

Which answers letters; which knows the way
The money goes, which deals with dentists

And Road Fund Tax and meeting trains,
And postcards to the lonely; which upholds

The permanently rickety elaborate
Structures of living; which is Atlas.

And maintenance is the sensible side of love,
Which knows what time and weather are doing
To my brickwork; insulates my faulty wiring;
Laughs at my dryrotten jokes; remembers
My need for gloss and grouting; which keeps
My suspect edifice upright in the air,
As Atlas did the sky.

CHAPLAINCY FELL WALK

There is always one out in front
With superior calves and experienced boots;

Always a final pair to be waited for,
Not saying much, pale, rather fat;

And the holy ones in the middle, making it
Their part to acclimatize the lonely and new,
Introducing cinquefoil, a heron, a view;

And a stout one who giggles, uniting us
In wonder at her unfaltering chokes;
But alarming too. For what is she laughing at?

And remote presence of hills;
And the absence of you.

CHRISTMAS PRESENTS

Christmas, very, have a merry very
A very merry Christmas, trilled the cards.
In gynae wards that means: There is a future.

I lay there, while you sorted friends and stamps.
The local wise man had come up with gold:
A benign cluster. You'll be home by Christmas.

Nothing to say. When I was tired, we held hands.

But next bed's visitors were staring.
Why us? The colour of our hair, perhaps?

You didn't notice, so I didn't tell you.

Next day (another day!) her bed was stripped.

Her lovers (husband? daughter?) hadn't cared
To watch death creeping up and down her face;
Stared at us out of tact, no doubt,
Somewhere to rest their smarting eyes, but also
(I like to think) because we were,
Of all things, human;

Human, of all things.

COMING TO

Swimming out of dreams
Still following the imperative
Cyphers of darkness; exchanging blindly
Warm clothes for cold, sleep-walking through
The up-to-date electricity of breakfast;
Two ages modulate into
A manageable present only as you
Shut the front door.

CONFESSIO AMANTIS

Because I know who you are
Up to a point: – you are
Martha, who feels ashamed
Of merely doing; Atlas
Who uncomplaining keeps off the fearful
Skies from the cringing earth
With the palms of his hands
For ever, without mentioning it, so that he appears
To be a mountain rather than a man;
Martha, the handyman of the Lord,
Up to a point;
     therefore to you
I will confess my own name. I am Dog
Who loves mankind but must also
Bark at the gate; I am Dragon,
Mythical, absurd, with wings; I am also

Watchman, who waketh, generally without a clue
Of what he waketh for; and I am Spy,
Watchman's other self, the double agent,
The fifth column who has lost touch
With the other four. And I am the fifth column
(Which is unnecessary) who is the Fool,
Full of wise saws and modern instances,
Babbling away irrelevant, incoherent,
In the world's apocalyptic thunderstorm

Up to a point.

The custom of the country
Is carnival. The currency
Civility. The dialect,
A dated demotic.

The country's creed is cheerful:
Sursum corda its canticle.
No benefit of clergy, but
Love never lies bleeding.

What chronicler conveys its
Uncalculating comedy?
What calligraphy comprehends
Centaurs and calypsos?

The cuisine is catholic
And kind. Congruity counts for
More than conformity. Chaucer
And Shakespeare its classics.

Cartographers cannot dis-
Cover these contours. The cautious
Citizens only acknowledge
You king of the castle.

DEAR TRUE LOVE

Leaping and dancing
Means to-ing and fro-ing:
Drummers and pipers –
Loud banging and blowing;
Even a pear-tree
Needs room to grow in

Goose eggs and gold top
When I'm trying to slim?
And seven swans swimming?
Where could they swim?

Mine is a small house,
Your gifts are grand;
One ring at a time
Is enough for this hand.

Hens, colly birds, doves –
A gastronome's treat.
But love, I did tell you,
I've given up meat.

Your fairy-tale presents
Are wasted on me.
Just send me your love
And set all the birds free.

DEAR VALENTINE

I know my limits.
I can't rig the lottery for you
(Though maybe a small two-way bet on the two-thirty at Southwell ...).

I've put in an order for foxes
At ease on their ground, where you can watch
As long as daylight; buzzards mewing downhill,
And posing for you at the proper distance;
The collared couple mooning and cooing
At that familiar address;

And I'm working on a meal you haven't had to imagine,
A house cleaned to the rafters, and humming
With order, scent, colour;

Lastly, the big thing, a canvas ready,
Light and shape occurring to the eye
For the hand to take further;
And dog, cats, me
Anticipating your every wish.

DIFFICILIOR LECTIO

'thaes ofereode, thisses swa maeg' (Deor)

Absence is incontinent. It leaves
Shaming wet patches in obvious places.
Some people cry easily. I am one.

Not you.

Study of Old English, under legendary masters,
I took to be an advantage. So many years later
That all I can safely remember is a *hwaet* or so,
I can't eliminate the aura of authority,

Claim to understand the ancestral mind,
How it was always defeat that moved them; how, if the hero
Killed a dragon or two, there was always
A final one coming; how to be on the winning side

Was dull, and also misleading. You, who read translations,
Speak humbly of their world. I catch you
House-training the dragon, my absence, with small
Jokes, diet of liver and onions, digging
A vegetable patch, reading my old books.

Why, I ask, *why the Anglo-Saxons?*

Because, you said, *they understand exile.*

DIGLIS LOCK

Image of something unknown: dank walls
Where nothing grows but chains; moody
Unreadable water; dog howling near;
Keeper unseen; but we are scrutinised
From above. Then the great gates open
To let us through, and in the half-darkness
I hardly see you, but I know you are smiling.

Yours was the needlework, precise and painful
As claws on a loved naked shoulder, that sewed us
Back into that Merthyr morning, when, terrorised by tod-
dlers,
You mined under our alien gateway, claimed sanctuary
In a jacket pocket.

You were the first to join our outlandish outfit
On that hilltop housing estate, with the garage-in-name-
only,
Invisible agog neighbours, rhubarb corms from Aberfan;
You the first source of our logged jokes, with
Your ears akimbo,

Eyes so excited they retreated behind their withers,
Living a paw-to-mouth existence, elbowing your way
Up bodies like a midshipman up rigging
Your whiskers wet with passion, sitting with one ear
In a human mouth, to keep warm.

I was never sure that English was your language,
Though you were probably just as dim in Welsh,
Vague about status, doglike coming to a whistle,
Running on white bandy-legs with a
Welcoming cluck.

You never took offence, were always ready
With an Eskimo kiss of your pink plebeian nose;
Set records for slow learning when we installed
The cat-flap; had no idea of the gravitas
Proper to cats.

Exiled in Gloucestershire, you domesticated
It for us, materialised on preoccupied laps, and,
Mozart-addict, rushed in filthy-footed from
Uprooting lupins, to settle yourself round Primo's collar
When duets began.

Now the heir's installed, she colonises
The outposts, (both next-doors, and one further)
Where she's feasted and feted. Such cunning
Is natural to your prudent race, in case
Of catastrophe.

And I see, dear dead one, how we severed you
From your own earth, how you chose us to be
Your territory. You are there quite often,
Dear tabby blur, in my bad eye's corner. We left you
Nothing to haunt but ourselves.

Haunt us still, dear first-footer,
First to live with us, first to confirm
Us as livers-together, you who took us so simply
For granted, translator of life into
The vernacular of love,
You who saw love, where innocent others
Saw only convenience.

ENVOY

You are the places that I've been to see:
The blue-eyed lochs, the eloquent and still
Air, the low-stranded clouds, the milky sea.
The map that turns from paper into hill,
Waterfall, corrie, at a moment's gaze,
The enterprises that we didn't do,
The gentle nights, the boot-and-sock-clad days –
I don't need them at home, for I have you.

And you are what I come back home to find:
The free dog ambling on the dew-grey grass;
Autumn bonfires; suburban gardens lined
With asters; letters; shops. Holidays pass,
Working-days, and weekends, as seasons do.
It doesn't matter. All of them are you.

FOR LEO ON 14.II.2000

Some whim of the calendar. For who
Could imagine the birds would woo
In mid-Feb, when we know quite well
That it's solstice-onwards that they do?

Some whim of the calendar. For who
But a martyr bishop that nobody knew
Would be linked with the business of kiss and tell
When a saucy young saintlet would do?

Ignoring the calendar, as I do,
Year in, year out, and leap-year too,
I may not love you especially well –
But I love you more dearly, I do.

All the same, I deplore the national neurosis
Which believes the best way to celebrate two hearts that beat as one is
A dozen long-stemmed martyred crimson roses.

FOR UA, IN CORNWALL

That it should be you –
Whose laugh,
Famously infectious,
Was worth a fortune
In any audience;

Whose scholarship,
So carelessly worn,
Amazed everyone
Who heard you;

Whose wit
Came from all directions,
Sudden and unexpected as spring;

That it should be you –
Whose wisdom should have advised you better;

Whose sense
Of self-preservation is so frail
You still can't see

How you're wasted on me.

GOING UNDER

I turn over pages, you say,
Louder than any woman in Europe.

But reading's my specific for keeping
Reality at bay; my lullaby.

You slip into sleep as fast
And neat as a dipper.
You lie there, breathing, breathing.

My language is turn over
Over and over again. I am a fish
Netted on a giveaway mattress,
Urgent to be out of the air.

Reading would help; or pills.
But light would wake you from your resolute
Progress through night.

The dreams waiting for me twitter and bleat.
All the things I ever did wrong
Queue by the bed in order of precedence,
Worst last.

Exhausted by guilt, I nuzzle
Your shoulder. Out lobs
A casual, heavy arm. You anchor me
In your own easy sound.

HEREBY

I hereby release you from time;
From the tyranny of small purpose-built rooms;
From crammed distressful lunch-breaks;
From *Coffeemate*. I divorce you
From the *you* that other people
Have decided you are; I restore to you
Sunday evenings. I have said
There shall be no more marking;
No more reading of uncongenial books
Just because they are on the syllabus;
No more explaining the worth of unparalleled poems
To unimpressed note-takers. No more endless
Phone calls after midnight about
Essay titles, references, girls. No more
Paranoid colleagues, no more
Torpid secretaries. Finally
I invest you with the month of September,
Which you were last able to attend to
At the age of four. Hereby I give you
All this, said the magician. Freedom, it's called.
Why aren't you pleased?

(early version of 'Hereby 2' published in
Collected Poems *as 'Now What?')*

HOMING IN

Somewhere overseas England are struggling
On a sticky wicket; somewhere in Europe
An elder statesman is dying *adagio;* and here,
Nowhere precisely, I slip to pips and bens
Through the occupied air.

Somewhere along this road an invisible ditch
Signals tribe's end, an important mutation of [^];
Somewhere among these implacable place-names
People are living coherent lives. For me the unfocussed
Landscape of exile.

Somewhere along this watershed weather
Will assert itself, swap wet for dry,
Scribble or flare on windscreens, send freak gusts
Sneaking round juggernauts, ravel traffic with
A long foggy finger.

Home starts at Birmingham. Places
Where I have walked are my auguries:
The stagey Malverns, watery sharp Bredon,
May Hill's arboreal quiff. These as I pass
Will bring me luck if they look my way.

I should be rehearsing contingencies,
Making resolutions, allowing for change
In the tricky minor modes of love. But,
Absorbed by nearly-home names,
Dear absurd Saul, Framilode, Frampton-on-Severn,

I drop, unprepared, into one particular
Parish, one street, one house, one you,
Exact, ignorant and faithful as swallows commuting
From Sahara to garage shelf.

IDYLL

Not knowing even that we're on the way,
Until suddenly we're there. How shall we know?

There will be blackbirds, in a late March evening,
Blur of woodsmoke, whisky in grand glasses,

A poem of yours, waiting to be read; and one of mine;
A reflective bitch, a cat materialised

On a knee. All fears of present and future
Will be over, all guilts forgiven.

Maybe, heaven. Or maybe
We can get so far in this world. I'll believe we can.

LOOKING FOR JORVIK

Veterans swap yarns about how long they queued
In the rain to see Tutankhamun.

Sweet summer York is nothing. They dip alertly
Into the dark, the time capsule. (*No dogs,*

Smoking, ice-cream, cameras.) History
Breathes them is, past *Pack up your troubles,*

Puffing billies, factory acts, perukes, Marston Moor,
(*Have you got a sweetie, Geoffrey love?*)

Mendicant friars, the Black Death, through the one
Date everybody knows, to the ancestral

Mutter and reek. This is then, now. We are
Where it was, it is. (*There's a man as big*

As a troll at the door.) Here the foundations are,
Pit, mud, stumps, the endless tons of bones,

Tiny dark plum stones of Viking York.
(And he said *I dabbled my blade in*

Bloodaxe's boy.) At this level the appalling
Icelander Egil who must not be killed at night

(*Night-killings are murder*) saved his neck by his
Head-Ransom song next day. And got off.

As we do, in the souvenir shop. *That wouldn't
Interest me. But for someone like Barbara,*

Who's a real intellectual . . . she was an English teacher,
You know. T shirts, baseball caps, keyrings, tapestry kits,

Activity packs proclaim *Eric Bloodaxe Rules OK.* And I
Have unearthed my own past under Jorvik's shaft,

Changing trains twenty years ago on York station at midnight
Among kit-bagged soldiers, on my way to you, thinking suddenly:

I am on my way to life.

Note:
In 948, Egil had been shipwrecked off the Yorkshire coast, and knew
he could expect no mercy from Eric Bloodaxe, who ruled York,
because he had killed Eric's son. The rules of that society prevented
Eric from having Egil put to death at once, because he had arrived
after dark, so Egil was given the task of composing overnight his
Head-Ransom song (20 stanzas in praise of Eric). This, because it
was so brilliant, forced Eric to grant Egil his life.

MATRIMONIAL POEM

I would get married on May Day at six
With the dog and the postman and milkman to cheer me
on
And back to a whisky and bacon and eggs
And then we'd be gone.

THE MINERAL LOVER

What do you make of this,
Sweetheart? I, who had been looking
For you all my long life, met
You when I was twenty-eight,
And didn't notice. We worked together
For seven casual years, till I discovered
I'd fallen in love with you
When I wasn't looking.

All very well
For Marvell to talk about vegetable loves, that
Grow vaster than empires and more
Slow. What about me?

MY LION IS A UNICORN

My lion is a unicorn.
He, sunbrowned and splendid,
Distributes love with lavish
Paws and growls goldenly.
She, tender-hoofed and weighed
Down with incongruous
Ivory lumber, shivers
With nerves, and is
Scared of virgins.

My lion is as strong as a
Ten ton truck. He tosses
Pancakes and cabers with his
Debonair tail. But my
Unicorn suffers from
Cold sores, hay fever and
A weak back, not to mention
Chilblains on the sensitive
Tip of her horn.

My lion is as hot as a
Boiling kettle. He hugs
Me to his royal mane and
Comforts me. But my sad
Unicorn creeps into
My bed and whimpers, *Please
Make me happy please make me
Happy.* Darling unicorn,
You need my lion
To comfort you.

The bookshop's golden cell retains the hours
Dictated by the abbey clock. Time swirls,
Clouding the paperbacks. We bob along
Caught by the tide. Elegant glossy books,
Out of our depth, veer to us on the swell,
But finally we drift ashore, and buy
Some recipes for stews at fifty pence.

Outside the Sherborne evening shines in cars'
Dipped beams, shop windows flame with pineapples
And Christmas cactus. Wood smoke fits its smell
Around the gleaming town. We turn aside
Past the no-entry sign. Night edges in.
You furl your sheepskin arm around my neck:
No one knows us here anyway. We walk
Laughing along the middle of the road.

The car is warm with dog. She licks our cheeks,
Liking the salty cold. We fold ourselves,
Coats, purchases, into the hairy nest.
We share a look. Reservoirs volley free
And shoot us level with the Dorset stars.

PER PRO

On behalf of Shandy
I am asked to say:
You are dandy,
Sugar-candy,
Spick-and-spandy,
Good as brandy
Or tokay;
And your mongrel wants to lick you,
Honour with her rhetoric you
On your special day.

On behalf of Mog,
This curt monologue:
I love you, Boss,
But to my loss
Know fewer words
Than mynah-birds
Or that loquacious demagogue,
Your dog.
Still, I can say
(Or purr)
Happy birthday, dear Boss,
I *love* yer.

On behalf of the house:
No rat, no mouse,
No moth, no rust,
No crud, no dust,
In Culverhay House.
Clock chimes,
Rose climbs,
Paint's bright,
Lock's tight,

My roof holds taut
All that you brought
And sought
And wrought.
I hold them fast under both sun and moon.
Hail, my new owner. Come back soon.

PIANO DUET

Sombrely you were drawn together in
that insoluble and hostile encounter:
a piano and you.
    Bella Akhmadulina, trans. Elaine Feinstein

Primo	I have the tune.
Secundo	That's all you're fit for.
	Counterpoint's subtleties are safe with me.
P	Your endless strumming drumming dulls the ear
	But it says nothing. Listeners must hear *me*.
S	This is my deep lugubrious bit.
	I must be heard above your treble squawk.
P	I *am* p p p p ing. Mind your feet.
	This is Mozart, not a country walk.
S	Wrong note. You should have played F sharp.
P	Is that a sharp? I took it for a natural.
S	No comment. Can't you hear how it should be?
P	I can. But I was fighting off your knee.
S	Now try again. *Sostenuto, allargando,*
P	*Con fuoco, presto, ritardando*
S	Too loud, too loud. Peace now. We've made it.
P	This is our music, and we've played it.

The Piano: Ah music, food of love ...

THE POET'S COMPANION

Must be in mint condition, not disposed
To hay fever, headaches, hangovers, hysteria, these being
The poet's prerogative.

Typing and shorthand desirable. Ability
To function on long walks and in fast trains an advantage.
Must be visible/invisible

At the drop of a dactyl. Should be either
A mobile dictionary, thesaurus and encyclopaedia,
Or have instant access to same.

Cordon bleu and accountancy skills essential,
Also cooking of figures and instant recall of names
Of once-met strangers.

Should keep a good address book. In public will lead
The laughter, applause, the unbearably moving silence.
Must sustain with grace

The role of Muse, with even more grace the existence
Of another eight or so, also camera's curious peeping
When the poet is reading a particularly

Randy poem about her, or (worse) about someone else.
Ability to endure reproaches for forgetfulness, lack of interest,
Heart, is looked for,

Also instant invention of convincing excuses for what the Poet
Does not want to do, and long-term ability to remember
Precise detail of each.

Must be personable, not beautiful. The Poet
Is not expected to waste time supervising
The Companion. She will bear

Charming, enchanted children, all of them
Variations on the Poet theme, and
Impossibly gifted.

Must travel well, be fluent in the more aesthetic
European languages; must be a Finder
Of nasty scraps of paper

And the miscellany of junk the Poet loses
And needs *this minute, now*. Must be well-read,
Well-earthed, well able

To forget her childhood's grand trajectory,
And sustain with undiminished poise
That saddest dedication: *lastly my wife*

Who did the typing.

POETRY READING: FOR LEO

Afterwards he swallows
Water. The skin round his lips
Is pale. He eyes us faintly.
He has emptied himself.

Is applause correct, or
Low? Uncertainly we clap.
Can this coarse act fit his spare lines?
Have we been kind, or crass?

He looks gently at us.
The qualifications of
Our response touch him. Tuned to his
Sharp string, we know he wants

Only to go away.
Whatever he says or we
Say will make no difference
To his aloof poems

Armed on the shining page.
But he, who is no longer
Their man, feels for them and for us
In our need to return

Him something. We can all
Hear the gross gaffes' heavy breath-
ing, as they wait their cue. You
Only were brave enough to bolt.

QUEUEING OUTSIDE THE JEU DE PAUME IN LIGHT RAIN

If you were here
I'd ask the smiling African
In my slow-motion French what makes his birds
Rattle their paper wings, and fly, and fall
Beside his hand. *Gilly-gilly-gilly,* he woos us all,
Very good, very nice. For you he'd laugh,
And tell.

If you were here
Something profound about his airy art,
The art we queue for under our umbrellas,
Would bounce between us, jokily. You'd note
The grace of our neighbours' passing-the-time conversation
(*Mind you, Muriel says it's always raining in Paris,*
And she lives here).

I have grown expert on your absences. I know
How things would differ, how the resolute
Mock-bird would tangle frailly with my feet,
And how you'd buy it, just because it did,
And you were there.

REFLECTION (1965)

Funny how I never get used to a mirror –
There I am and that is me,
And I'm hard to recognise;
Each time I've forgotten what I look like,
And am surprised
And disheartened.

Funny how I never get used to you.
Suddenly, with a shock of recognition
There you are, in my thought,
And I'd forgotten you were quite so serious,
So alarming, so gentle,
Made such concise ironic jokes.
To think of you is to see myself in the mirror
And find I'm nicer
Than I thought.

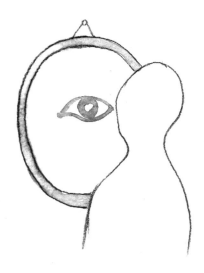

SKIN-LOOSE

The skin that separates me from the air
Isn't exactly me, though other people
Salute it as the demarcation line.

Inside my skin is me, they think. Outside,
A foot or so of space I like to keep
Clear for myself. Beyond that, open country.

That's how it ought to be, I know. But somehow
The open country got inside my skin.
There's a gap between me and my cortex,

And I feel cold in it. A chill wind
Of nonentity disturbs my spaces. My hands
Drop things, my feet can't follow music,

My ears won't listen to what is said
To me, my eyes aren't smart enough
To see through their own lenses.

But with you, my skin fits me as snugly
As the shining coat of an evergreen leaf,
And I dance in time to your music

SONG

Don't eavesdrop on my heart,
  It's a sneak.
It will chat with any stranger,
Lifeguard, lover, doctor, tailor;
It just needs to feel an ear
  And it will speak.

Don't cavesdrop on my heart,
  It's illiterate.
The educated hand, eye, brain,
Turn words to shapes and back again;
My stupid heart could never learn
  The alphabet.

Don't eavcsdrop on my heart,
  It's dumb.
In rainforests of tubes and pumps
It hangs, my heart, a third-world dunce;
Parrots can speak, but my heart just
  Communicates by drum.

Don't eavcsdrop on my heart,
  It's clever.
And if your head should touch my breast
My heart would make its own arrest,
Develop hands, as trees grow leaves,
  And hold you there forever.

19 August: Two days designed to become special. *Look,*
Said the novelist to herself, *at the present moment.*

For ten days this heat has lasted (96 degrees)
In London, hottest day of the year.

And up in Northumberland, waiting for its
Own public moment, in its fluid temperate zone,

The baby nearly born; novelist in London watching;
Baby in the north waiting, sharing the one,

The particular moment. Friday, in Bloomsbury,
Girls and young men lying in white on the grass.

20 August: And Saturday, Saturday was the day
When the clouds came, and a wind blew,

And the baby decided that the moment was now
After all those months, and set about coming.

And there was lightning, Mozart spat and fizzed
On the radio, and down in Sussex everybody

Like prisoners escaped – dogs bounding,
Horses galloping, wind blowing – everything released

And *Look,* said the novelist to herself, *at*
The present moment, and *Look,* said the baby to the company,

This is me, I am here. And the baby
Came into the world at that particular moment

Which is precious for me because it brought you with it;
Precious to the world because Virginia Woolf said *Look,*
And Leonard was staking out the dewpond,
And Virginia saw an old vagabond playing with flowers
Under a furze-bush, and Rosie said sleepily
Up in Northumberland, *I've come to join all this.*

TO TO

The ones I care for most
Are the unambitious monosyllables

(*Of, to, by, with* and *from, now* and *then,*
And *and*, of course)

That stitch sentences and thoughts together.
Without them, nouns and verbs at loggerheads.

These are the words that shoulder sense,
That are taken for granted; these are the ones

That poets blue-pencil; they are
Repetitive as hiccups, getting no glory,

Mere working-class words, on which
The pattern of things depends. It was you,

Leo, who taught me to see the small
Self-effacers, without which, chaos.

Thank you for *before* and *after, you, me,* and *us,*
The leap-frogging mites that lead to the best things there are –
The glad ding-dong of verbs: *Look. Like. Listen.*
Love.

ULLAPOOL

Low houses cram themselves along the spit.
Monstrous fish-heads snarl upwards from the quay.
I watch you squeeze the past to make it fit
The newer Ullapool you didn't see.
The smells co-operate, but other things,
Distorted mirrors of their older selves,
Tease with obliquity. Memory clings
Along these toad-flaxed walls, these gift-shop shelves,
Stroking you with a clammy fingertip,
Abrupt reminder of a mood or tone,
Though grocers' shops and gardens tend to slip
From where you left them. I must chaperone
You between then and now. And privately
Hope to make this a dear memory.

WHERE'ER I WALK

Cradled in your thoughts
I become
The magic lady that you see.

Buds pop out like springs
As I pass,
Tall trees bend to bless me with leaves,

Old men see visions,
Babies laugh,
Cats crave the touch of my fingers,

Birds especially
Celebrate
My coming among them with song.

Dear, I am only
A mortal,
To whom silence, punctures, sorrow,

False notes, stones in shoes,
Clumsiness
Of hand and spirit must happen.

In your eyes I am
Enchanted.
I love to be held in your cat's

Cradle of love, but
Let me keep
My immortal feet on the ground.

WITH YOU

I stand with you in the garden
The birds' surprising madrigals
Rise through the roar of bees.

I stand with you in the kitchen
Dear damaged long loved over-used
Pans and pots protect us.

I stand with you in the hallway
With the deep oak tick of the clock
And the turning stair.

We sit by books in the lamplight
Importunate nondescript dog and cat
Surround us warmly.

We lie in the lofty bedroom
The church clock through the window
Quartering Gloucestershire silences.

Without you, no garden.
Sunshine withers on the plum tree
House shrinks derelict into dust.

WORKSHOP'S END

True happiness consists not in a multitude of friends,
but in their worth and choice.   (Dr Johnson)

In the old stories, when the band
At last dissolves, they go their separate ways,
Robin, the Friar, Maid Marian and the rest,
The merry men. I'm desolate.
I want them all to stay together,
Whatever the weather,
For ever.

I know they can't. They've other lives to lead,
Must marry, emigrate, turn respectable,
But in my head they're still walking the greenwood
Together, for ever. The last pages
Are never opened.

Now our last page. Year by year we've walked
The enchanted workshop ground: the dark magician;
The Yorkshire truth-teller; the humble one
Who thought she couldn't do it; me. We have explored
Bravely, in difficult places. We've laughed a lot.
We've loved, not thinking much about it.
We've stayed together,
We thought, for ever.

Now no more. Well, things do end,
However much I like to think they don't.
But we shall keep this rare and sideways knowledge
Of you, of you, of you and me,
Effect of workshop camaraderie
Together. In these poems,
Whatever the weather,
It lasts for ever.

YOU

who
 make lists and then lose them
 eat kosher wine gums and jelly babies
 have to have gloves on the shortest journeys
 lose your gloves
 are always thirsty
 love to laugh
 are so easily moved to tears
 yawn more loudly than anyone else in the world
 can sleep at the drop of a hat
 love mussels and scallops
 love lobster and crabs
 never eat lobster and crabs because they suffer so

whose glasses always need polishing

who never have a hanky to polish your glasses
 always have at least four pens in your pocket in case a poem
   should occur
 have no colour sense whatsoever
 love wild flowers and know the songs of birds
 collect binoculars and never use them
 love torches of every kind
 love maps, old churches, rivers
 love swimming but never swim
 hate carrots and all root veg
 love dogs
 adore cats
 would like to own a snake
 hate hot weather
 hate being cold
 love fizzy lemonade
 forget PIN numbers

How could anyone resist you?

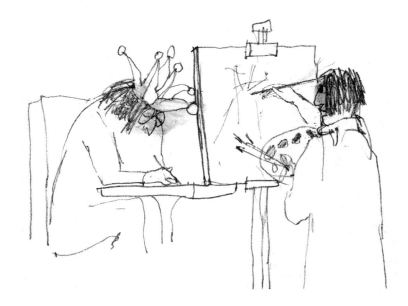

7301

Learning to read you, twenty years ago,
Over the pub lunch cheese-and-onion rolls.

Learning you eat raw onions; learning your taste
For obscurity, how you encode teachers and classrooms

As the hands, the shop-floor; learning to hide
The sudden shining naked looks of love. And thinking

The rest of our lives, the rest of our lives
Doing perfectly ordinary things together – riding

In buses, walking in Sainsbury's, sitting
In pubs eating cheese-and-onion rolls,

All those tomorrows. Now twenty years after,
We've had seventy-three hundred of them, and

(If your arithmetic's right, and our luck) we may
Fairly reckon on seventy-three hundred more.

I hold them crammed in my arms, colossal crops
Of shining tomorrows that may never happen,

But may they! Still learning to read you,
To hear what it is you're saying, to master the code.